BOMBAY
LUNCHBOX

भारत गैस स्टाल

हमारे यहाँ स्टोव
गैशबत्ती बैटरी
लाइटर किफायती
भाव से रिपेरिंग
किये जाते है
गेश बत्ती भौंड

Gulab

Singh

भाप
चाय होबल
दूध नेबू फुल गलास
दूध फिका
नेश कोफी

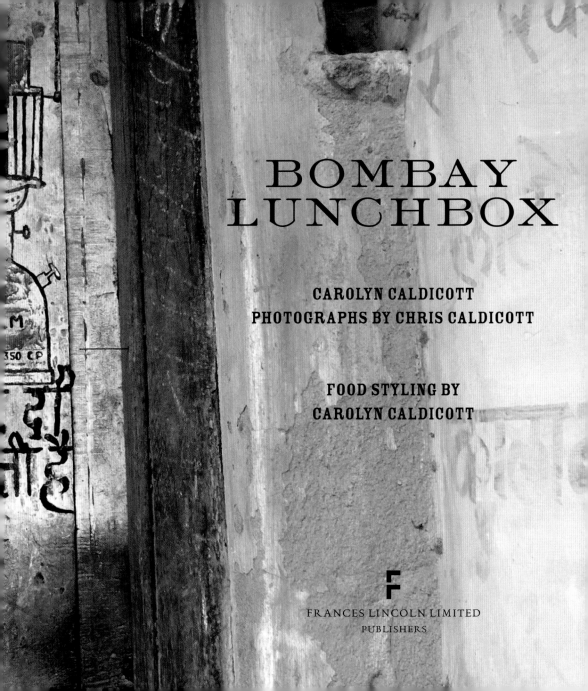

BOMBAY LUNCHBOX

CAROLYN CALDICOTT
PHOTOGRAPHS BY CHRIS CALDICOTT

FOOD STYLING BY
CAROLYN CALDICOTT

F
FRANCES LINCOLN LIMITED
PUBLISHERS

CONTENTS

HOW TIFFIN CAME ABOUT

W hen the British established themselves in India in the late eighteenth century, it soon became clear that adaptation was needed. For a start, the rituals of eating were going to have to change to accommodate the hot, languid days and nights. In the heat of the day lunch became a much lighter meal — but what to call it? Somehow, the word that seemed to stick was 'tiffin', taken from the slang words 'tiff', a tot of diluted liquor, and 'tiffing', to take a sip of this liquor (perhaps a hint that a sahib's lunch might quite often be of the liquid variety!). Tiffin took off and 'a spot of tiffin' soon became a peg on which almost any culinary indulgence between breakfast and dinner could be hung.

From these origins in British India tiffin has evolved to create a fascinating world of its own, a world that involves a whole range of dishes and equipment and above all of suppliers, from the tiffinwallahs of Bombay to the sellers of spiced tea and savoury snacks who cater for busy punters on the run. Today tiffin might mean a packed lunchbox or afternoon tea, a savoury snack or a sweet treat. As long as it is munched between breakfast and dinner, it is simply tiffin.

CLASSIC ANGLO-INDIAN FAVOURITES

*A*nd then – what to eat? Young wives arrived in India completely inexperienced to the ways of this 'new' life, clutching copies of books giving all manner of advice (most completely impractical) on how to run a household overseas. Baffled by the lady of the house's demands for bland meat and two veg, cook reached a compromise and devised unique dishes that combined Indian traditional cuisine with ingredients and spicing more suited to the British palate.

Turmeric, cumin, coriander, ginger and garlic were combined with pepper, nutmeg, mace and bay – spices and herbs popular in England at the time – with the addition of yoghurt, ground nuts and coconut to help reduce pungency. At first dishes tended to be mild, but as British palates became more accustomed to the new taste sensations their cooks got more adventurous, adding cayenne and chilli to the pot.

In turn the British back home embraced these exciting new flavours from India. Curry powder made its way to British shores, and spicy chutneys and piccalilli became all the rage. Famously, Queen Victoria employed an Indian chef. The Hindustani Coffee House opened its doors in 1809 on a fashionable London square, serving a selection of curries to new converts eager to try Indian cuisine and old hands missing the piquant taste of their travels. By the mid-nineteenth century curry had become so popular that William Makepeace Thackeray penned a poem to it and fashionable cookbooks pronounced that 'few dinners are thought to be complete without [a curry] on the table'.

CURRY POWDER

Curry powder as we know it today was invented when British officers keen to take a taste of India home with them requested merchants of the bazaar to mix a general concoction of spices that could be pre-roasted, ground and tightly packaged for the long journey. The original mix was based on a South Indian combination that traditionally included ground curry leaves, hence the name curry powder.

CURRY

There are various stories about the origins of the name 'curry', but it is usually thought to have evolved from the Tamil word for spicy sauce – *kari*. The term became an all-encompassing name for any stew or even dry preparation that included spices. The first curry recipe in English was printed in 1747 under the title 'How to Make a Curry the Indian Way'.

CAFE DIPAC
P. D. MORAJKAR
Mapusa Goa Bastora

PEPPER

Did you know pepper grows on a perennial vine and is pollinated by monsoon rainwater? Native to the Malabar Coast of India, pepper, with its wonderful ability to stimulate the taste buds and make even a dull dish enjoyable, became one of the most important spices traded on the spice routes.

MULLIGATAWNY SOUP

Created to feed the insatiable English appetite for soup, mulligatawny is thought to have originated from Tamil milagu thannir (chilli pepper water), a thin peppery dhal. There are many different recipes for mulligatawny. You can also add chunks of cooked chicken along with the rice.

SERVES 6

200g/7oz red split lentils
1 tablespoon ghee or butter
1 medium onion, finely chopped
3 cloves garlic, finely chopped
4cm/1½ inch piece of ginger root,
    peeled and grated
1 red chilli, sliced
2 teaspoons ground coriander
2 teaspoons ground cumin
1 teaspoon ground turmeric
½ teaspoon black pepper
1 teaspoon garam masala
1 large apple, cubed

2 carrots, cubed
4 sticks celery, cubed
1½ litres/2½ pints water
½ teaspoon ground cardamom
225ml/8 fl oz thick coconut milk
juice of half a lemon
a handful of finely chopped coriander
    leaves
1 teacup cooked basmati rice
salt

To garnish: chopped coriander leaves

Rinse the lentils until the water runs clear, then set them to one side until ready to use.

Melt the ghee in a medium-sized saucepan. Add the onion, garlic, ginger and chilli and sauté together until the onion becomes translucent.

Combine the spices and stir into the onion mixture. Stir-fry for a minute or so before adding the apple, carrots and celery. Continue to stir-fry until they start to soften.

Add the lentils and cover with the water. Bring the pan to the boil, then reduce the heat and gently simmer until the lentils are soft and breaking down (discarding any foam that rises to the surface and stirring occasionally to prevent sticking).

Finally stir in the cooked rice, coconut milk, lemon juice, chopped coriander leaves and salt to taste. Gently simmer for a further 5 minutes to allow the flavours to combine. Serve garnished with chopped coriander leaves.

PEPPER CHICKEN WITH MANGO RAITA

Serve this simple but delicious dish of stir-fried pepper chicken with mango raita and a dollop of Major Grey's chutney (page 27).

SERVES 4–6

PEPPER CHICKEN
4 free-range chicken breasts
2 generous tablespoons sunflower oil
1 large red onion, finely sliced
2 cloves garlic, crushed
1 teaspoon cracked black pepper
½ teaspoon ground turmeric
salt

MANGO RAITA
225g/8oz natural yoghurt
1 teaspoon cumin seeds
½ smallish mango, peeled and diced
small handful chopped mint leaves
a good squeeze of lime juice
1 teaspoon runny honey
salt

To garnish: mango slices, extra chopped mint
and roasted cumin seed and finely diced red onion

To prepare the raita, whisk the yoghurt until smooth, then dry-roast the cumin seeds in a hot pan for a minute or so and stir into the yoghurt along with the remaining ingredients. Season with salt to taste and chill in the fridge until ready to use.

Cut the chicken breasts into strips and season with salt to taste.

Heat the sunflower oil in a wok. When the oil is sizzling hot add the onion and garlic and stir-fry until soft.

Add the sliced chicken and stir-fry until browned on all sides. Stir in the pepper and turmeric, and when the chicken is completely coated in the spices, add a splash of water (approximately 55ml/2fl oz). Continue to stir-fry until the water has reduced, the onions are caramelized and the chicken is dry but still tender.

Spoon the raita over the chicken and top with mango slices, chopped mint, and a sprinkling of cumin seeds and diced red onion.

EGG CURRY

Eggs and potatoes simmered in a rich tomato curry sauce is a rather excellent legacy of the British Empire. Serve with chapatti or rice.

SERVES 4–6

1 medium onion, roughly chopped
2 garlic cloves, roughly chopped
3cm/1¼ inch fresh ginger root, peeled
    and roughly chopped
2 teaspoons ground turmeric
½ teaspoon chilli flakes
6 free-range eggs, hard-boiled
4 tablespoons sunflower oil
3 medium waxy potatoes, peeled
    and diced

1 medium red onion, finely sliced
1 small cinnamon stick
6 cardamom pods, slit
6 cloves
4 bay leaves
3 medium tomatoes, diced
275ml/½ pint water
1 teaspoon jaggery or soft brown sugar
salt and pepper

Blend the roughly chopped onion, garlic and ginger in a food processor until a paste forms. Stir in the turmeric and chilli flakes and set to one side.

Peel the hard-boiled eggs and slash the whites a few times with a knife. Cut the eggs in half lengthwise.

Heat the oil in a wok or large frying pan. When it is hot fry the eggs until golden. Remove the eggs from the pan and set to one side.

Add the diced potato to the same pan and stir-fry until brown. Scoop the potatoes from the pan with a slotted spoon and set to one side.

Fry the sliced red onion in the oil remaining in the wok. When the onion becomes translucent add the cinnamon, cardamom, cloves and bay leaves, stir-fry for a further minute or so, then add the onion spice mix and stir-fry until soft.

Add the chopped tomatoes and cook for 5 minutes before stirring in the water, fried potatoes and jaggery. Season the sauce to taste with salt and a good grind of black pepper, lay the eggs on top (yolks up) and gently simmer until the sauce is reduced and the potatoes are soft.

SUNDAY ROAST ANGLO-INDIAN STYLE

Even the essential Sunday roast had a make-over. Chicken was marinated tandoori -style with yoghurt, lime and spices, then stuffed with spiced potatoes. The roast would typically be served with paratha, but mixed vegetables work just as well.

SERVES 4–6

1.35 kg/3lb free-range chicken
2 garlic cloves
1cm/½ inch piece fresh ginger,
 peeled and roughly chopped
2 tablespoons natural yoghurt
2 tablespoons lime juice
½ teaspoon ground chilli
½ teaspoon ground turmeric
salt
sunflower oil

To serve: a handful of chopped
 coriander leaves

POTATO STUFFING
3 tablespoons sunflower oil
½ teaspoon cumin seeds
1 medium onion, finely chopped
2 garlic cloves, finely chopped
1 teaspoon ground coriander
1 scant teaspoon ground cumin
1 scant teaspoon garam masala
3 medium waxy potatoes,
 peeled and diced
1 teaspoon lime juice
salt and black pepper

Rinse the chicken cavity with water and drain well.

To make the marinade, blend the garlic and ginger in a food processor until a paste forms. Combine the paste with the yoghurt, lime juice, chilli and turmeric, and season with salt to taste.

Rub the marinade over the outside of the chicken, cover with foil and store in the fridge for 2 hours.

To prepare the stuffing, heat the sunflower oil in a large frying pan, add the cumin seeds and as soon as the seeds start to crackle add the chopped onion and garlic and stir-fry until the onion starts to soften.

Stir in the remaining spices and cook for a minute or so before adding the diced potatoes. Continue to stir-fry until the potatoes start to soften and brown. Add the lemon juice and season with salt and pepper to taste. Allow the stuffing to cool a little before handling.

Preheat the oven to 190°C/375°F/gas mark 6

Place the chicken in a roasting tin and pack the stuffing into its cavity. Drizzle the chicken with a little sunflower oil and place in the preheated oven for 1¼–1½ hours. To check the chicken is cooked insert a carving fork into the thickest part of the leg: if the juices run clear it is ready.

Cover the chicken with foil and allow to rest for 10 minutes before carving. Scoop the stuffing into a warm bowl, and serve alongside the chicken sprinkled with chopped coriander.

RAILWAY LAMB CURRY

This classic Anglo-Indian dish full of aromatic spices was famously served in the smart Railway Refreshment Rooms on board the trains that crossed India. The elegant dining car tables were laid with crisp white linen and china and attended by turbaned waiters.

Traditionally it was mutton that was simmered in the spiced onion gravy, with tamarind water or vinegar added as a preserving agent. I like to use lamb chops and balsamic vinegar (and I always serve the chops with a pink tinge in the middle).

SERVES 4–6

6 medium-sized lamb chops
3 garlic cloves
2.5cm/1 inch piece fresh ginger, peeled
salt
½ teaspoon ground chilli
3 tablespoons sunflower oil
10 curry leaves
6 peppercorns
6 cloves
6 cardamom pods, crushed

3 dried red chillies, broken into large pieces
2 medium onions, finely sliced
1 teaspoon ground coriander
1 teaspoon paprika
½ teaspoon ground cumin
2 tablespoons balsamic vinegar
150ml/¼ pint water
150ml/¼ pint coconut milk
salt

Using a pestle and mortar, blend the garlic and ginger with a good pinch of salt until a paste forms. Set half the paste to one side. Combine the remaining half with the ground chilli. Rub this paste over the chops and leave to marinate for half an hour or so.

Heat the sunflower oil in a large frying pan. When the oil is really hot brown the chops on both sides.

Remove the chops from the pan and add the curry leaves, peppercorns, cloves, cardamom and chillies. Fry for a minute or so before adding the sliced onions and the remaining garlic/ginger paste. Fry together, stirring constantly, until the onions are soft. Stir in the ground coriander, paprika and cumin, and return the chops to the pan.

Add the vinegar and allow it to reduce a little before adding the water. Give the pan a good stir and simmer gently until the gravy has thickened a little. Add the coconut milk and continue to cook until the chops are cooked tthrough and the sauce is thick and rich. Adjust the seasoning before serving.

KEDGEREE

A perfect example of the mishmash of flavours that characterized Anglo-Indian cuisine, kedgeree is loosely based on khichri, a comforting, mildly spiced rice and lentil dish. The lentils were promptly replaced by fish and hard-boiled eggs, ingredients more suited to the British taste. Kedgeree became immensely popular as a breakfast dish in Victorian England, and it was here that the recipe was further enhanced by the addition of smoked haddock.

SERVES 4

4 large free-range eggs
2 teacups basmati rice
1 cinnamon stick
450g/1lb white fish or undyed
   smoked haddock
2 bay leaves
½ teaspoon black peppercorns
3 good tablespoons unsalted butter
1 large red onion, finely sliced

½ teaspoon ground coriander
½ teaspoon ground cumin
½ teaspoon ground turmeric
¼ teaspoon ground cardamom
chilli flakes to taste
a handful of chopped coriander leaves
salt and black pepper
a large lemon cut into wedges

Boil the eggs in simmering water for 10 minutes, remove from the pan and immerse immediately in cold water until cool (this ensure the yolks stay a nice bright yellow). Peel the eggs and cut into bite-sized chunks.

Wash the rice until the water runs clear, place in a saucepan and cover with 4 teacups of cold water. Add the cinnamon stick and bring the rice to the boil. Reduce the heat, cover the pan and gently simmer until the rice has absorbed all the water. Turn off the heat and allow the rice to sit for 5 minutes before fluffing with a fork.

Lay the fish in the bottom of a frying pan and cover with boiling water. Add the bay leaves and peppercorns and gently simmer together for 5 minutes. Remove the fish from the pan and allow it to cool a little before flaking into chunks (discarding any rogue skin or bones you come across).

Heat the butter in a large non-stick frying pan. When the butter starts to foam add the chopped onion and sauté until the onions caramelize. Stir in the spices and cook for a minute or so before adding the cooked rice. Stir-fry until the rice is evenly coated with the spice mixture and heated through.

Gently combine the flaked fish and chopped coriander with the rice over a low heat. Season the kedgeree to taste and served topped with the chopped boiled egg and the lemon wedges.

MASALA FRIED FISH

Not quite battered fish, but certainly just as good, in fact possibly even better!

SERVES 4
4 smallish pomfret or mackerel, or
    4 fish fillets such as pollock,
    haddock or cod
sunflower oil to fry

THE MASALA PASTE
2 cm/¾ inch piece of cinnamon stick
1 teaspoon coriander seeds
½ teaspoon cumin seeds

½ teaspoon black peppercorns
¼ teaspoon fennel seeds
3 shallots, roughly chopped
3 garlic cloves
2 cm/1½ inch piece fresh ginger
    root, peeled and roughy chopped
2 medium tomatoes, roughly chopped

To serve: lemon wedges

Slash the fish a couple of times with a sharp knife and rub the turmeric, chilli, salt and lemon juice into the flesh. Set to one side for half an hour.

While the fish is marinating, prepare the masala paste. Dry-roast the whole spices in a hot pan for a couple of minutes, until they become aromatic. Then, using a pestle and mortar, grind then together to make a powder. Combine the ground spices with the remaining masala paste ingredients and blend in a food processor until a paste forms.

Cover the fish with the paste and leave to marinate for a further 10 minutes.

Generously coat the fish with semolina and heat a good glug of sunflower oil in a non-stick frying pan. When the oil is sizzling hot, fry the fish fillets until golden brown and crunchy on both sides.

Serve immediately with a squeeze of lemon.

BEETROOT AND COCONUT MILK CURRY

Beetroot, considered quite a delicacy in Victorian England, was cultivated in India to combine with curries and salads to invoke memories of home. If you want to avoid pink-stained hands, always wear rubber gloves when preparing beetroot.

SERVES 4–6 AS A SIDE DISH

3 tablespoons sunflower oil
1 teaspoon black mustard seeds
1 red onion, diced
3 garlic cloves, crushed
2 red chillies, finely chopped
2 bay leaves
5 cloves
1 cinnamon stick, broken into 3 pieces
½ teaspoon ground turmeric
450g/1lb raw beetroot, peeled and diced
3 medium tomatoes, finely diced
150ml/¼ pint coconut milk
juice of a lime
salt

Heat the sunflower oil in a heavy-bottomed saucepan and when it is sizzling hot add the mustard seeds. As the seeds start to pop, add the onion, garlic and chilli, and stir-fry until soft.

Add the bay leaves, cloves, cinnamon and turmeric and stir-fry with the onion mixture for a minute or so before adding the beetroot. When the beetroot is well coated in the spices, add the chopped tomatoes and 275ml/½ pint of water.

Season with salt to taste, cover the pan and gently simmer until the beetroot is soft. Stir in the coconut milk and the lime juice and continue to simmer until the sauce has thickened.

CHUTNEY

Salty or sweet, dry or jam-like, chatni traditionally accompanies most meals in India. The British rather took a shine to these perky preserves, made from a combination of fruit and vegetables simmered with spices, dried fruit, vinegar and sugar. With a tweak here and there chatni was transformed into chutney. And who today could imagine a ploughman's without chutney?

MAJOR GREY'S MANGO CHUTNEY

Legend has it that in the nineteenth century an English officer in the Bengal Lancers created this mildly spiced sweet chutney with the help of his Bengali cook. It rapidly became a firm favourite in India, and jars soon found their way to London. Crosse & Blackwell cannily copied the recipe and Major Grey's Mango Chutney became the luxury preserve of choice in fashionable circles.

MAKES ABOUT 4 JARS
4 medium-sized firm mangoes, peeled and diced
1 whole lemon (including the skin),
   deseeded and finely diced
1 large onion, diced
2 garlic cloves, crushed
75g/3oz golden raisins
50g/2oz ginger root peeled and grated
175g/6oz soft brown sugar

150g/5oz molasses
1 generous teaspoon mustard seeds
1 teaspoon chilli flakes
1 teaspoon ground coriander
½ teaspoon cracked black pepper
½ teaspoon ground nutmeg
¼ teaspoon ground clove
1 cinnamon stick
275ml/½ pint cider vinegar

Combine all the ingredients in a non-reactive saucepan and warm together over a medium heat until the sugar and molasses have dissolved. Increase the heat to bring the pan to a gentle simmer. Continue to simmer, stirring regularly, until the chutney has a jam-like consistency. Ladle into sterilized jars and allow to mature for at least a month before opening.

CREAMY CARDAMOM AND SAFFRON RICE PUDDING

Rice pudding with an exotic twist, ambrosia of the gods! In India jaggery (palm sugar) is traditionally used to sweeten this milky pudding. If you can't track jaggery down, soft brown sugar makes a good substitute.

SERVES 4–6
1 litre/1¾ pints full-fat milk
50g/2oz basmati rice, rinsed
3 bay leaves
a good pinch of saffron
1 scant teaspoon ground cardamom
a handful of golden raisins
a handful each of flaked almonds and
    cashew nut halves
1 tablespoon rose water
jaggery or soft brown sugar

Pour the milk into a heavy-bottomed pan and gently heat until boiling point is nearly reached. Add the rice, bay leaves and saffron, and gently simmer (stirring occasionally to prevent sticking) until the rice is soft, the milk has reduced by half and the pudding has a creamy texture.

Remove the bay leaves and stir in the ground cardamom, raisins, nuts (keeping a few nuts back to garnish the pudding) and rose water. Sweeten to taste with jaggery or brown sugar and simmer for a further few minutes. Serve hot or cold, sprinkled with the rest of the nuts.

LUNCH IN A BOX

The word Tiffin is also used as a name for a lunchbox. Tiffins (or dhabbas) come in all shapes and sizes, but traditionally they are round, with three or four stacking stainless steel compartments firmly sealed with a tight-fitting lid and a side clip to avoid any nasty spillages and a handle for carrying on top.

In India food cooked at home with care and love is considered to deliver not only healthy (and relatively cheap) food but also divine contentment. Lunch is usually eaten thali-style, with a tantalizing selection of regional delicacies that may include any combination of spicy vegetables, dhal, rice, yoghurt, pickles, bread and pudding served on a big steel plate or a banana leaf. The separate compartments in the tiffin luchbox accommodate thali lunches perfectly.

Tiffin culture is now to be found all over India. Everyone – from women in brightly coloured saris working in the fields to giggling families on long train journeys – carries a tiffin to provide a compact, portable, home-made lunch.

THE TIFFINWALLAHS OF BOMBAY AND THEIR
HOT HOME-COOKED CARGO

Every weekday without fail something rather extraordinary is to be seen around midday on the chaotic streets of Bombay (or Mumbai). This is the sight of hundreds of stainless steel tiered tiffin boxes or dhabbas piled high on hand carts and bicycles being pushed through the streets by dhoti-wearing, white-capped tiffinwallahs.

　　Expertly run by the Mumbai Tiffin Box Suppliers' Association, armies of these tiffinwallahs provide the invaluable daily service of speedily delivering piping-hot home-cooked lunches to over 200,000 busy office workers. Many workers live 50 kilometres or more from their workplace, a long commute on a packed train. There is certainly not time for the cook of the

house to prepare a full meal before they leave home. So the lunch-filled tiffin boxes are picked up later in the morning, colour-coded and transported to the station, where they are collected by the tiffinwallahs, whose mission is to deliver each box to its corresponding workplace still hot from the pan – and to return the empty tiffin to the home before the end of the working day. With the essential core values of punctuality, teamwork, honesty and sincerity providing the backbone to the business, they have a staggering 99.99% success rate.

The barely literate tiffinwallahs have become so revered that they are now called on to lecture to big businesses, and have been honoured guests at British royal weddings. They are considered so trustworthy that workers often place their wages inside the clean tiffin box on its return journey rather than risk carrying money on the commuter train.

RED LENTIL DHAL WITH MIXED SPICE TADKA

Dhal, a simple pulse-based dish tempered with fried whole spices (or tadka) may be served just with rice and pickle or as part of a more elaborate thali.

SERVES 4–6
2 cups split red lentils, rinsed
1½ litres/2½ pints water
a thumb-sized piece of ginger root,
    peeled and grated
1 teaspoon ground turmeric
salt and ground black pepper

THE TADKA
2 tablespoons ghee, butter or
    sunflower oil
1 dessertspoon mustard seeds
1 heaped teaspoon cumin seeds
4 red chillies, slit lengthwise and
    deseeded

Wash the lentils until the water runs clear, place in a medium-sized saucepan, cover with
    the measured quantity of water and stir in the grated ginger and turmeric.
Bring to the boil (scooping off any foam that rises to the surface), then reduce the heat and
    gently simmer until the the lentils are soft and breaking down. Turn off the heat.
To prepare the tadka, heat the ghee in a small frying pan. When it begins to foam

add the mustard and cumin seeds and the chillis. As the seeds start to pop pour the tadka on top of the dhal (standing back as the ghee will splutter). Season to taste and simmer for a few minutes longer to allow the flavours to combine.

Serve with basmati rice and pickles.

SAAG PANEER

Creamy spinach studded with golden cubes of paneer, if you prefer a lighter option use yoghurt in place of cream.

Paneer is a non-melting fresh cheese made by curdling milk with lemon juice. The curds are wrapped in a cloth and placed under a heavy weight to remove any excess whey. The resulting firm cheese is then cut into cubes for cooking.

SERVES 4–6

1 kg/2lb 4oz spinach, finely sliced
3 tablespoons ghee or butter
350g/12oz paneer, cut into cubes
1 heaped teaspoon garam masala
1 scant teaspoon cayenne pepper
salt
1 small onion, roughly chopped

5cm/2 inch piece of peeled ginger root, roughly chopped
4 garlic cloves
3 green chillies
225ml/7 fl oz double cream or natural yoghurt
large handful of fenugreek or coriander leaves, roughly chopped (optional)

Place the sliced spinach in a large saucepan, add a splash of water (just enough to stop the spinach sticking) and simmer for a few minutes until the spinach wilts. Pour off any excess water (leaving a little still clinging to the leaves) and set to one side.

Heat the ghee in a medium-sized saucepan and fry the paneer cubes until they are golden brown on all sides. Using a slotted spoon, remove the paneer from the pan. Place it on a large flat plate and sprinkle with the garam masala, cayenne pepper and salt to taste.

Blend the onion, ginger, garlic and chilli in a food processor until finely chopped. Fry the vegetable mixture in the hot ghee remaining in the saucepan until soft.

Add the cooked spinach and marinated paneer, cover the pan and simmer together for 10 minutes (stirring regularly and adding a little water if necessary).

Stir in the cream and the chopped fenugreek and gently simmer for a further 5 minutes. Finally, adjust the seasoning to taste.

ALOO GOBI

Classic tiffin tucker at its best.

SERVES 4–6

4 tablespoons sunflower oil
2 teaspoons fennel seeds
1 teaspoon fenugreek seeds
1 large onion, diced
2 or 3 red chillies, finely chopped
4cm/1½ inch piece ginger root,
    peeled and finely chopped
4 garlic cloves, crushed
1 small bunch coriander, stalks finely
    chopped and leaves roughly chopped

2 medium potatoes, peeled and diced
1 teaspoon ground turmeric
1 smallish cauliflower, cut into florets
4 medium tomatoes, diced
2 teaspoons garam masala
1 teaspoon chopped jaggery or honey
salt

To garnish: fresh ginger root and
    red chill julienne

Heat the oil in a heavy-bottomed saucepan. When it is sizzling hot add the fennel and fenugreek seeds. As the seeds start to crackle add the onion, chilli, ginger, garlic and coriander stalks. Stir-fry until the onion is soft.

Add the diced potatoes and continue to stir-fry until the potatoes start to soften. Stir in the turmeric. Add the cauliflower florets and give the pan a good stir.

When the cauliflower is well coated with spices, add the tomato and a good splash of water. Stir in the garam masala and jaggery and season with salt.

Cover the pan and gently simmer until the vegetables are soft. Add the coriander leaves just before serving. Garnish with the ginger and chilli julienne.

CHANA MASALA

This protein-packed chickpea and sweet potato curry is particularly good served with mango raita (page 13).

SERVES 4–6

4 tablespoons ghee, butter or
   sunflower oil
1 teaspoon black mustard seeds
2 medium red onions, diced
4 garlic cloves, crushed
3cm/1¼ inch piece ginger root,
   peeled and finely chopped
2 fresh red chillies, finely chopped
2 dried red chillies
2 teaspoons ground coriander
1 teaspoon ground cumin
½ teaspoon ground turmeric

1 medium sweet potato,
   peeled and diced
3 carrots, peeled and diced
2 x 400g/14oz tin chickpeas,
   drained and rinsed
3 heaped tablespoons tomato purée
1 cinnamon stick
250g/9oz coconut milk
1 teaspoon garam masala
salt

To serve: thinly sliced red onion;
   chopped coriander; lemon wedges

Heat the ghee in a heavy-bottomed saucepan. When it starts to foam add the mustard seeds. As the seeds start to pop add the onion, garlic and chilli and stir-fry until soft.

Stir in the ground coriander, cumin and turmeric and fry for a few seconds before adding the diced sweet potato and carrot. Continue to stir-fry until the vegetables start to brown.

Add the drained chickpeas, tomato purée and cinnamon and stir in enough water to make a thickish gravy. Cover the pan and gently simmer, stirring regularly until the vegetables are just soft.

Add the coconut milk, garam masala and salt to taste. Gently simmer together for a further 5 minutes or so to allow the flavours to combine and the sauce to thicken.

Serve topped with sliced red onion, chopped coriander and a squeeze of lemon juice.

POTATO AND FRESH PEA CURRY

New potatoes and fresh peas in an easy-to-prepare tiffin curry.

SERVES 4–6

600g/1lb 5oz diced baby new potatoes
½ teaspoon ground turmeric
4 tablespoons sunflower oil
2 teaspoons black mustard seeds
14 curry leaves
1 large onion, diced
4cm/1½ inch piece ginger root,
    peeled and finely chopped

4 garlic cloves, crushed
3 green chillies, finely chopped
2 teaspoons ground coriander
400g/14oz tin chopped tomatoes
225g/8oz shelled fresh peas
salt
2 teaspoons garam masala

Place the potatoes in a medium-sized pan with the ground turmeric and add enough water to cover. Bring the pan to the boil, reduce the heat and simmer until the potatoes are just soft. Drain the potatoes, retaining 2 teacups of the cooking water, and set to one side for later.

Heat the oil in a large wok. When it is really hot, add the mustard seeds, then as the seeds start to pop stir in the curry leaves, onion, ginger, garlic and chilli and stir-fry together until the onion is soft but not brown.

Stir in the ground coriander and cooked diced potatoes. When the potatoes are coated with spice, stir in the tomatoes, the peas and the retained cooking water.

Season with salt to taste and gently simmer until the peas are cooked and the sauce has thickened. Finally, stir in the garam masala and simmer for a further couple of minutes before serving.

GOAN CHILLI FRIED PRAWNS

Marinated prawns dipped in semolina and shallow-fried.

MAKES 20
20 large raw prawns, de-veined
coarse semolina to coat the prawns
sunflower oil to shallow-fry

THE MARINADE
1 scant teaspoon ground turmeric
1 teaspoon ground chilli (or to taste)
½ teaspoon ground cumin
2 garlic cloves, crushed

1cm/½ inch piece ginger root,
     peeled and grated
½ teaspoon tamarind
     concentrate (optional)
2 tablespoons lime juice
salt

To serve: lime wedges

Combine the marinade ingredients together in a bowl, add the de-veined prawns and gently mix together until the prawns are well coated. Leave the prawns to marinate for half an hour.

Pour a teacup of semolina into a small bowl and roll the marinated prawns in the semolina until evenly coated (topping up the bowl if necessary).

Coat the bottom of a non-stick frying pan with sunflower oil, heat until sizzling hot and fry the prawns in batches until golden brown on both sides.

Serve with a squeeze of lime juice.

BEETROOT STIR-FRY TOPPED WITH AUBERGINE, FETA CHEESE AND TURMERIC OIL DRESSING

Serve hot or cold with chapatti and mixed salad leaves.

SERVES 4–6

1 medium aubergine, thinly sliced
salt
½ teaspoon ground turmeric
sunflower oil
1 heaped teaspoon black mustard seeds
15 curry leaves
1 medium red onion, cut in half and
    thinly sliced
2cm/1¼ inch piece ginger root,
    peeled and grated
2 garlic cloves, finely chopped
2 red chillies, finely chopped

3 medium beetroot, peeled and cut
    into fat matchsticks
250g/9oz feta cheese, cut into cubes
110g/4oz chopped walnuts
a handful of chopped coriander leaves

TURMERIC OIL DRESSING
3 tablespoons olive oil
¼ teaspoon ground turmeric
1 tablespoon lime juice
salt and freshly ground black pepper

Place the sliced aubergine in a colander, sprinkle with a little salt and set to one side for half an hour to drain. Pat the slices dry with kitchen paper and sprinkle with ground turmeric. Heat a good measure of sunflower oil in a wok and fry the aubergine slices until brown on both sides.

In the same wok, add a dash more sunflower oil and fry the mustard seeds until they start to pop. Add the curry leaves, onion, ginger, garlic and chilli and stir-fry until soft. Add the beetroot and continue to stir-fry until it is just soft.

To prepare the turmeric oil dressing, gently heat the olive oil and turmeric together until the turmeric has dissolved, add the lime juice and season with salt and freshly ground black pepper to taste.

To serve, top the stir-fry with fried aubergine slices and feta cheese, sprinkle with chopped walnuts and coriander leaves and drizzle with the turmeric oil dressing.

RAITAS

A chilled yoghurt-based raita will cool even the hottest curry.

FRESH MINT AND CUCUMBER RAITA

SERVES 4–6

250g/9oz natural yoghurt
half a medium cucumber, peeled,
    deseeded and grated
1cm/½ inch piece ginger root,
    peeled and grated

a small handful of mint leaves,
    finely chopped
¼ teaspoon roasted ground cumin
¼ teaspoon ground black pepper
salt

Whip the yoghurt with a fork until smooth. Combine the whipped yoghurt with the remaining ingredients and chill in the fridge until ready to serve.

PAPAYA AND DATE RAITA

SERVES 4–6

250g/9oz natural yoghurt
1 teaspoon mustard seeds
2 tablespoons desiccated coconut
half a firm smallish-sized papaya,
    peeled, deseeded and grated

3 soft fresh dates, finely chopped
a small handful of coriander leaves,
    finely chopped
¼ teaspoon ground ginger
1 teaspoon honey
salt

Whip the yoghurt with a fork until smooth.

Dry-roast the mustard seeds in a hot frying pan. When they start to pop, add the desiccated coconut and continue to roast for a few minutes longer until the coconut turns golden brown. Allow to cool a little before combining with the yoghurt.

Stir in the remaining ingredients and chill in the fridge before serving.

AFTERNOON TIFFIN

***

*T*he quintessential British tradition of afternoon tea was very quickly assimilated into India's culinary day. Afternoon tiffin filled the gap between lunch and dinner with a cup of delicate home-grown orange pekoe tea, savouries and sweet treats. Spicy snacks were added to the tiered cake stand, with little dishes of fiery chutney to accompany them. Coriander and mint chutney made its way into delicate cucumber sandwiches and fresh ginger into cakes. Cooks couldn't resist adding a pinch of cardamom to scones and a dash of rose water to scent the cream to top them. Strawberries were cultivated in the cooler climes of hill stations to make the all-important strawberry jam. For officers out in the field afternoon tiffin would be packaged and beautifully served on location.

TEA

An insatiable desire for tea played a large part in the British presence in India. In a bid to break the Chinese monopoly in the tea trade, smuggled seeds from China were germinated in Calcutta's botanical gardens and transported to the hills of Assam and Darjeeling to be cultivated. The resulting tea from Assam produced a strong, robust brew, whereas Darjeeling, with its perfect combination of wet, warm climate and altitude, produced a delicate, superior tea that quickly became considered 'the champagne of teas'. Plantations and trade soon flourished and fortunes were made.

Tea has subsequently become the lifeblood of India. Scented with spices, it is consumed copiously from Kashmir to Calcutta. It is drunk as 'bed tea' first thing in the morning, served with meals, offered to guests in homes or as a bargaining tool in the market. It is brewed all day in makeshift stalls on street corners and at teatime in smart hotels. Whether poured from elegant bone china teapots, sipped from hand-thrown clay cups, or gulped down in *dharbas* by truck drivers, it is the great egalitarian refreshment of India.

DARJEELING TEA

To appreciate to the full the light, fragrant taste of the 'champagne of teas' it is essential to serve the tea black and unadulterated.

'First flush' Darjeeling, small young leaves picked in mid-march after the spring rains, makes the most refined brew. The later 'second flush' has an amber colour and a more full-bodied taste. Later in the year the tea becomes progressively poorer in quality.

To make the perfect cup of tea add 1 teaspoon of Darjeeling tea leaves to a warmed pot and cover with hot – but not boiling – water. Allow the leaves to infuse for 3 minutes, then strain the tea into a second warmed pot. The leaves can then be used for a second infusion.

CUCUMBER SANDWICHES SPIKED
WITH SPICY MINT AND CORIANDER CHUTNEY

Classic cucumber sandwiches with an Indian twist. There is definitely an art to the perfect cucumber sandwich: it is essential that the bread is very fresh, crustless and thinly cut; and the cucumber must be salted to make sure it is firm and crisp.

SERVES 4–6
½ large cucumber
fine sea salt
12 thin slices of bread cut from
    a large sandwich loaf
soft butter

FOR THE MINT AND CORIANDER CHUTNEY
a large handful of coriander leaves
a large handful of mint leaves
1 or 2 green chillies, finely chopped
1 tablespoon lemon juice
1 scant teaspoon ground cumin
salt

Peel the cucumber and slice in paper-thin rounds. Place the slices in a colander, sprinkle with a little sea salt and allow to drain for 15 minutes.

While the cucumber is draining, prepare the chutney. Place all the chutney ingredients in a food processor and blend until smooth (adding a small dash of water if necessary).

Pat the cucumber slices dry with kitchen paper.

Thinly butter the bread slices, and spread 6 slices with chutney. Cover the chutney with 2 layers of cucumber and gently press the remaining slices of buttered bread on top.

Cut away the crusts with a bread knife and cut the sandwiches into triangles. Serve immediately if you can, as the bread does tend to dry out quite quickly. If you have to wait, cover the sandwiches with a damp tea towel or cling film until ready to serve.

CARROT, CHEESE AND TOMATO CHUTNEY SANDWICHES

Mix equal quantities of grated carrot and cheddar cheese with a sprinkling of chopped coriander leaves, add a shake of chaat masala and season to taste. Cut thin slices of brown bread and spread with butter and home-made tomato chutney (above). Cover half of the slices with the carrot and cheese mixture. Top with the remaining slices. Cut away the crusts and cut into delicate finger sandwiches.

INSTANT TOMATO CHUTNEY

SERVES 4–6

3 tablespoons sunflower oil
1 teaspoon cumin seeds
1 teaspoon black mustard seeds
½ teaspoon nigella seeds
1 garlic clove, finely chopped
½–1 teaspoon chilli flakes

6 ripe medium-sized tomatoes,
 finely diced
¼ teaspoon ground black pepper
1 teaspoon honey
Salt

Heat the oil in a small frying pan, when hot add the seeds, as they start to crackle, add the garlic and chilli and cook until the garlic becomes brown and crunchy.
 Stir in the chopped tomatoes, honey, black pepper and salt to taste. Cover the pan and gently simmer until the tomatoes break down and the chutney thickens.

TIFFIN TIME
2·00PM - 2·30PM

SPECIAL MASALA TEA

DARJEELING ASSAM NILGIRI K

TEA TEA TEA T

KASHMIRI GREEN TEA

VISHNU EMPORIUM TEA

INDIAN COFFEE HOUSE

WORKING HOUR :-

12·00   To 8·00 P.M.

MINI SAVOURIES

Dainty versions of favourite tiffin snacks are exactly the right size to serve for afternoon tiffin time, just enough to tempt the appetite without sabotaging it for dinner.

MINI KHASTA KACHORIS

Mini khasta kachoris (see page 120) are also rather good at teatime, try substituting the lentils with fresh peas for a lighter teatime filling.

MINI UTTAPAM

Uttapam look a little like a cross between a crumpet and a pancake. Made from a mixture of rice and urad dhal flour, they are topped with diced chilli, tomato, onion and coriander and served with coconut chutney.

Ready-mixed uttapam flour is available from Asian stores. If you can't find it, ready-mixed dosa flour will work just as well – or you can always mix your own. Traditionally the batter is fermented overnight, but the addition of baking powder makes an instant short cut.

SERVES 4-6

225g/8oz uttapam flour or dosa
   (or 150g rice flour combined with
   75g/3oz urad dhal flour)
1 teaspoon caster sugar
salt
2 tablespoons natural yoghurt
1 rounded teaspoon baking powder

3 medium tomatoes, finely chopped
1 smallish red onion, finely chopped
3 green chillies, finely chopped
a large handful coriander leaves,
   finely chopped
sunflower oil to fry

To serve: coconut chutney (see p68)

Sift the flour into a bowl and add the sugar and a good pinch of salt. Make a well in the middle of the flour and gradually stir in enough water to make a thick batter, crushing any lumps as you do so.

Beat in the yoghurt and baking powder until the batter becomes light and frothy. Add the chopped tomato, red onion, chilli and coriander and set to one side for 10 minutes.

Coat a flat griddle or non-stick frying pan with a little oil and heat on the stove until hot enough to make a drop of water sizzle. Take a ladle of the mixture and pour into 3 portions on the hot griddle. Use the back of a spoon to spread the batter into plump mini pancakes.

When bubbles form and the batter has set, turn the uttapam and cook the remaining side. Repeat the cooking process until all the batter has been used up. Serve warm with a spoonful of coconut chutney.

COCONUT CHUTNEY

75g/3oz freshly grated coconut
    or desiccated coconut
2.5cm/1inch piece peeled and
    grated ginger root
2 green chillies, finely chopped
2 tablespoons lemon juice
3 tablespoons natural yoghurt
1 teaspoon honey
salt

THE TEMPERING
1 tablespoon sunflower oil
1 teaspoon black mustard seeds
¼ teaspoon cracked
    black peppercorns
10 curry leaves

Blend the coconut, ginger, chilli, lemon juice, yoghurt and honey in a food processor until smooth. Season with salt to taste and scoop into a serving bowl.

To temper the chutney: heat the sunflower oil in a small frying pan. When it is really hot add the mustard seeds. As the seeds start to pop, add the cracked pepper and the curry leaves and cook for half a minute or so. Tip the mixture on top of the chutney.

FRESH LIME SODA

On a sultry afternoon a cooling lime soda makes a wonderful accompaniment to savoury snacks. It has been described as 'the supreme quencher of colonial thirst'. Traditionally a little salt is also added to the soda and sugar syrup is used as a sweetener.

To make sugar syrup, mix equal quantities of sugar and water in a small pan and warm together over a low heat until the sugar has dissolved. Allow the syrup to cool and store in the fridge until needed.

PER PERSON
1 lime
a thin slice of peeled ginger root
a slice of lemon
caster sugar
2 tablespoons sugar syrup or to taste
¼ teaspoon salt (optional)
ice
soda water
a small handful of fresh mint

Rub the fresh ginger and the lemon around the rim of a tall glass. Dip the rim into caster sugar – enough to give it a good coating.

Squeeze the lime and cut the skins into chunks. Place both juice and skin in the bottom of the glass and add sugar syrup and salt to taste.

DAINTY DHOKLA

This light, spongy savoury snack with a zingy topping is ideal to serve at teatime.

Dhokla is made from steamed chickpea flour batter. If you don't possess a steamer big enough, place a stand in a large saucepan (with a fitted lid), add water until it reaches halfway up the stand and bring the water to simmering point. Place the dhokla on the stand and cover the pan to cook.

Chickpea flour or besan is available from Asian stores, health food shops and good supermarkets.

SERVES 4–6
150g/5oz chickpea flour
½ teaspoon ground turmeric
1 teaspoon caster sugar
½ teaspoon salt
juice of a lemon
1 teaspoon finely grated ginger root
1 heaped teaspoon bicarbonate of soda

THE TEMPERING
2 tablespoons sunflower oil
3 green chillies, finely sliced
2 teaspoons black mustard seeds
1 teaspoon sesame seeds
10 curry leaves
1 heaped tablespoon desiccated coconut

To garnish: a handful of chopped coriander leaves, a little extra desiccated coconut and date and tamarind chutney (page 89)

Grease a 23cm/9inch cake tin or heatproof dish with a little sunflower oil. Put water to heat in a steamer or a large saucepan with a stand.

Sift the chickpea flour and turmeric into a mixing bowl. Make a well in the middle of the flour and gradually stir in 200ml/7fl oz warm water, crushing any lumps as you stir. Add the caster sugar, salt, lemon juice and ginger and at the last minute add the bicarbonate of soda. Pour immediately into the prepared tin.

Carefully lower the tin on to the stand; cover the pan and steam for 15 minutes (a cocktail stick inserted in the middle should come out clean). Remove the dhokla from the pan, allow to cool for 10 minutes, and then cut into bite-sized diamond shapes.

To make the tempering, heat the sunflower oil in a frying pan and when the oil is really hot add the sliced chilli followed by the mustard seeds. As the mustard seeds start to pop add the sesame seeds, curry leaves and desiccated coconut. Continue to fry until the coconut becomes golden. Add 4 tablespoons of warm water (this will splutter a little so stand back!) and pour evenly over the top of the dhokla.

Sprinkle the dhokla with chopped coriander leaves and a little extra coconut. Serve with date and tamarind chutney alongside, for dipping.

MINI SAMOSAS

Samosas are the perfect size to 'bridge that gap'. Street stalls and cafés offer freshly made samosas ready and waiting. Samosas are simply inseparable from masala chai; together they are a marriage made in heaven.

If you prefer a healthier alternative to fried samosas, bake on a greaseproof tray in an oven preheated to 200°C/400°F for 15 minutes or so, until golden brown.

MAKES ABOUT 18

225g/ 8oz ready-made shortcrust pastry
1 medium mashing potato
   (approx 250g/9oz), peeled and diced
2 tablespoons sunflower oil
1 teaspoon cumin seeds
1 medium onion, diced

3 green chillies, finely chopped
1 teaspoon garam masala
½ teaspoon ground cumin
50g/2oz fresh or frozen peas
salt
sunflower oil for deep-frying

Boil the diced potatoes in salted water until soft. Drain and roughly mash the potatoes until they start to break down, but are not completely smooth.

Heat the oil in a small frying pan. Add the cumin seeds and when they start to crackle, add the onion and chilli. Fry together until the onion is soft.

Add the garam masala, ground cumin and peas, stir- fry for a few minutes and then stur in the mashed potato. Tip the filling into a bowl and set to one side to cool.

To assemble the samosas, roll out the pastry on to a lightly floured surface until thinnish, but still thick enough to handle without breaking up. Cut into 10cm/4inch rounds, then cut each round in half to make a semicircle. Take a semicircle of pastry, wet the edges, fold in the straight edges to make a cone shape and pinch the edges together to ensure a good seal. Fill the pastry cone with a generous teaspoon of the potato/pea mixture and seal the remaining edges together. Repeat the process until all the ingredients have been used up.

Heat enough sunflower oil in a wok to deep-fry the samosas, and fry in batches of 6 until golden brown. Allow the samosas to drain on kitchen paper before serving.

GINGERBREAD

A moist, rich, gingery sponge that matures beautifully overnight. Spread with butter or serve just as it comes.

150g/ 5oz soft butter
110g/ 4oz soft brown sugar
1 large free-range egg, beaten
225ml/7 fl oz half/half mixture of treacle and honey
300g/11oz plain flour
1 heaped teaspoon bicarbonate of soda
2 teaspoons ground ginger
2 teaspoons grated ginger root
1 teaspoon cinnamon
½ teaspoon ground cloves
250ml/9fl oz warm full-fat milk

Line a 23cm/9inch square baking tin with greaseproof paper and preheat the oven to 180°C/350°F.

Beat the butter and sugar together until creamy and light. Beat in the egg followed by the treacle/honey mixture.

Sift the flour, bicarbonate of soda and spices into a bowl and gradually combine with the cake mixture. Stir in the warm milk and tip the mixture into the lined cake tin.

Bake the gingerbread in the preheated oven for 1 hour (a cocktail stick inserted in the middle of the cake should come out clean).

When the cake tin is cool enough to handle, carefully turn out and peel away the greaseproof paper. Leave the gingerbread to cool completely on a cake rack before cutting into dainty squares.

CARDAMOM SCONES

Serve these mini scones warm from the oven with a dollop of strawberry jam and rose-scented cream.

MAKES ABOUT 18

225g/8oz self raising flour
½ teaspoon baking powder
1 teaspoon ground cardamom
a pinch of salt
75g/3oz soft butter, cut into small cubes

25g/1oz caster sugar
1 large free-range egg
75ml/2fl oz whole milk
To serve: strawberry jam;
  rose-scented cream

Preheat the oven to 220°C/425°F/gas mark 7

Sift the flour, baking powder, cardamom and salt into a mixing bowl, add the soft butter and rub together until breadcrumbs form.

Beat the egg and milk together. Set 1 dessertspoon of the mixture to one side for later, then lightly combine the rest with the flour mixture until a soft dough forms (to prevent scones becoming heavy take care to not overwork the dough at this stage).

Roll out on to a floured surface until 2.5cm/1inch thick. Cut into 4cm/1½ inch rounds and place on a non-stick baking tray.

Brush the scones with the reserved egg/milk mixture and bake for 10–15 minutes, until golden brown and well risen.

ROSE-SCENTED CREAM

To make the rose-scented cream simply whip double cream until floppy peaks form and fold in icing sugar and rose water to taste.

BUTTERY SHREWSBURYS

There is an other-worldly air about Bombay's Irani cafés, with their bentwood chairs, marble-topped tables and mirrored walls, serenaded by the tick -tock from a pendulum clock. Their famous baked goods have a distinctly British feel, pillowy soft bread and rolls, Madeira cake and apple pie and the 'Best Shrewsburys in Town'. Named after the Shropshire town of their origin, Shrewsbury biscuits are still popular all over India. Try dunking these lemony shortbread-style biscuits into thick Irani chai made with an extra spoonful of condensed milk.

MAKES ABOUT 20

110g/4oz soft butter
150g/5oz caster sugar
   (plus extra to sprinkle on top)
2 free-range egg yolks

225g/8oz sifted plain flour
1 teaspoon baking powder
the grated zest of an unwaxed lemon
1teaspoon caraway seeds

Preheat the oven to 180ºC/350ºF/gas mark 4.

Beat the butter and sugar together until light and fluffy. Beat in the egg yolks one by one until well combined.

Add the sifted flour, baking powder, lemon zest and caraway seeds and gently mix together to make a stiff dough.

Roll out the dough on a lightly floured surface until a generous 0.5cm/¼ inch thick. Cut into 6cm/2½ inch rounds and place on a greased non-stick baking tray.

Bake in the preheated oven for 15 minutes or so, until golden brown. Sprinkle with a little extra caster sugar and transfer to a wire rack to cool.

KASHMIRI SAFFRON TEA

In the cooler temperatures of the hills of Kashmir, aromatic saffron tea is brewed to ward off colds. The clear golden nectar is poured over flaked almonds. As a variation on the recipe, you can add 2 teaspoons of green tea leaves to the liquid halfway through the brewing time.

SERVES 4–6
1 litre/1¾ pints water
3 good pinches saffron
1 cinnamon stick
8 cardamom pods, crushed
honey to taste
3 tablespoons flaked almonds
honey, to taste

Combine the water, saffron, cinnamon and cardamom in a saucepan. Bring the water to the boil, then reduce the heat, cover the pan, and gently simmer for 10 minutes.

To serve, add a teaspoon of flaked almonds to each cup and pour the tea on to. Sweeten with honey to taste.

CARROT HALWA

Sweet stalls piled high with colourful confections in all shapes and sizes make it almost impossible to pass by without making a purchase. Indian sweets – a heady mix of milk, buttery ghee, sugar and nuts simmered with rose water and cardamom – are not for the faint-hearted. At festival times huge boxes are filled to take home for the celebrations. At teatime a more modest square or two makes a naughty but nice accompaniment to a cup of tea.

Carrot halwa is slightly more virtuous and is served either hot or allowed to cool and cut into modest squares. Beetroot makes a dramatic variation on the recipe.

SERVES 4–6

3 tablespoons ghee or unsalted butter
50g/2oz cashew nuts
25g/1oz raw almonds, cut into slivers
250g/9oz grated carrot

570ml/1 pint full-fat milk
175g/6oz golden caster sugar
½ teaspoon ground cardamom

Melt the ghee in a thick-bottomed saucepan, add the cashews and almonds and toast until golden. Remove the nuts with a slotted spoon and set to one side.

Add the grated carrot and fry in the ghee until it starts to wilt. Stir in the milk and simmer until the milk has reduced by half.

Pour in the sugar and stir until it has completely dissolved. Add the cardamom and gently simmer (stirring regularly) until the milk has completely reduced and the carrots have a syrupy texture. Stir in the toasted nuts.

If you are allowing the halwa to cool, press the mixture into a greased square non-stick tin and place in the fridge to set. Cut into bite-sized squares to serve.

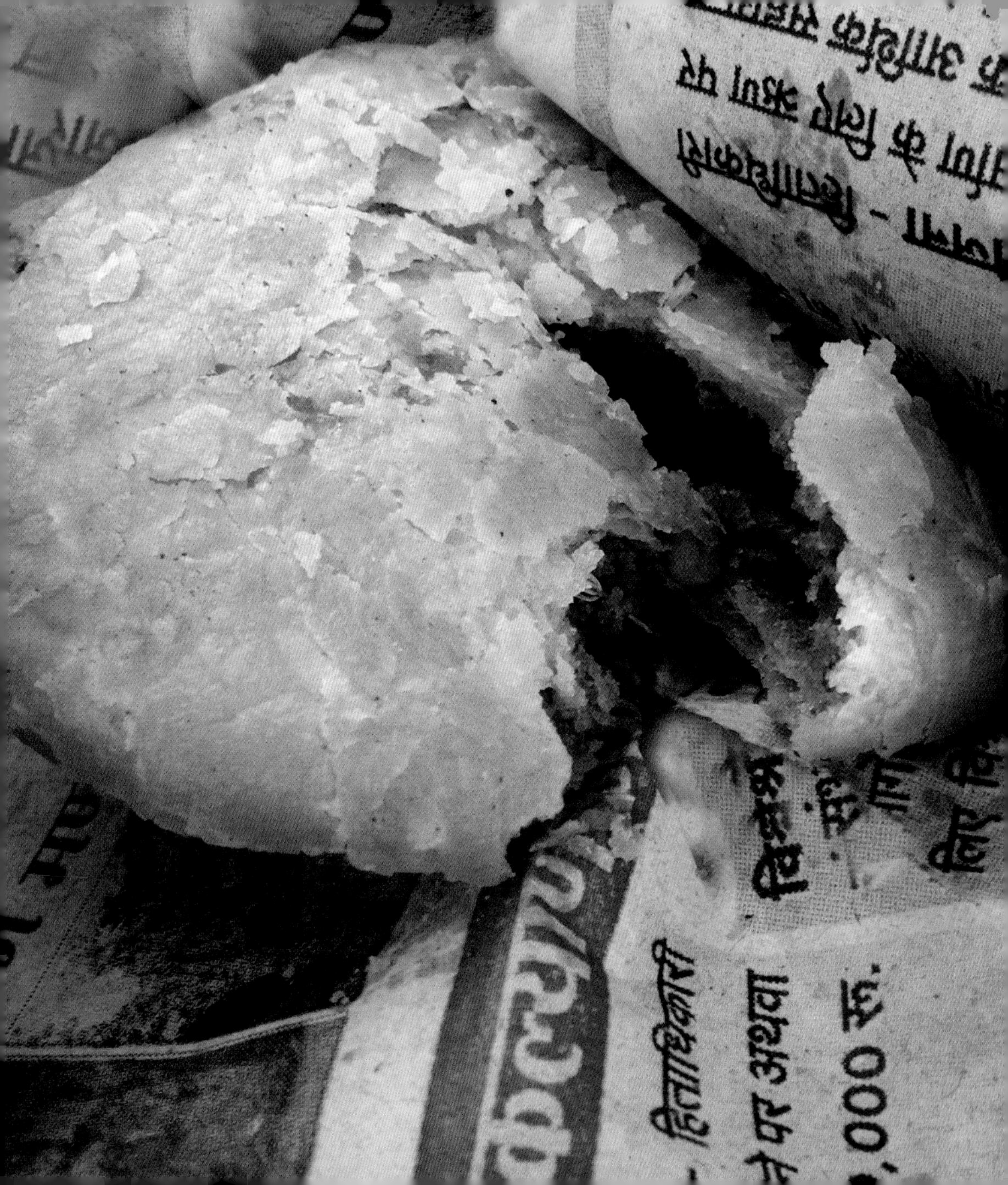

TIFFIN SNACKS

*I*ndians love to snack; snacking is ingrained in the culture. When hunger pangs hit, handy stalls selling all manner of delights will never be far away, making it possible to graze day and night on an almost endless choice of bite-sized morsels bursting with flavour.

At sunset families, friends and courting couples are drawn to the golden sands of Bombay's Chowpatty beach to sample its famous spicy savoury snacks. On the streets of Calcutta, busy office-workers stop off at simple hole in the wall cafés to grab a quick *kati* roll, expertly stuffed in front of their eyes with mouth-watering fillings. All over India, roadside *dhabas* offer weary travellers welcome sustenance in the form of freshly cooked favourites; a chance to stretch the legs, take in the local scene and return to the road refreshed. In villages and cities entrepreneurs erect makeshift stalls selling anything from chilli cheese toasties and masala pastry puffs to freshly squeezed sugar cane juice and creamy lassi. Roving vendors draw attention to their wares with a ring of a bell from the handlebars of a rickety bicycle or with a cry as they push a loaded handcart through the streets. Ice cream and fresh fruit, potato patties and chilli pakora are all on offer.

Bakeries and sweet shops, coffee houses and cafés, wherever a crowd gathers there will always be an array of mouth-watering tiffin on sale. Make the back-breaking climb to any hilltop temple and you can bet that you'll find steaming hot tea being being brewed at a chai stall at the summit. In the utmost depths of the countryside, as a train pulls into a sleepy station, basket-bearing traders will crowd the platform, tempting passengers with tantalizing home-made treats.

CHOWPATTY BEACH CHAATS

A carnival atmosphere pervades on Bombay's Chowpatty beach as the sun sets over the Arabian Sea. The perfect spot to take a stroll, have a paddle and, most importantly, snack. Legend has it that chaats (the generic term for snacks) such as bhel puri and dahl puri were invented here.

Most of the ingredients for puris are available ready-made from Asian shops. stock up your store cupboard and you will have a selection of tasty treats on tap.

YOU WILL NEED:
Sev (fried chickpea flour vermicelli)
Puffed rice
Puri (small hard round puffed pastry shells)
Roasted peanuts
Chaat masala spice mixture

DATE AND TAMARIND CHUTNEY

Date and tamarind chutney is served extensively as an accompaniment to snacks, salads and curries. It can be bought ready-made, but as it is so easy to make and stores well in the fridge for a couple of weeks, I always make my own.

MAKES 1 JAR

175g/6oz chopped dates
1 tablespoon tamarind concentrate
1 teaspoon ground cumin
1 teaspoon ground turmeric
½ teaspoon ground chilli
50g/2 oz brown sugar
275ml/ ½ pint water
salt

Place all the ingredients in a saucepan, bring the pan to the boil, reduce the heat to a minimum, cover the pan and gently simmer for 5 minutes.

Allow the mixture to cool, then place it in a food processor with a slash of cold water and blend until smooth. Store in an airtight container in the fridge.

SIMPLE CORIANDER CHUTNEY

SERVES 6

2 large handfuls of coriander leaves
1 green chilli, roughly chopped
1 teaspoon dry-roasted cumin powder
3 tablespoons lemon juice
salt

Blend all the ingredients in a food processor until finely chopped. Add a splash of water and blend again until smooth.

DAHI PURI

Bite-sized round pastry shells filled DIY-style with chopped potato, mung bean sprouts, chickpeas, chutney and yoghurt. Place all the ingredients in bowls on the table, fill a puri with what takes your fancy, and then pop into the mouth whole for an addictive taste explosion!

SERVES 4–6, 28 puri shells

THE PURI FILLING
1 medium waxy potato, peeled, diced and boiled until soft
half a red onion, diced
1 teacup cooked chickpeas
1 teacup mung bean sprouts
a good squeeze of lemon juice
1 teaspoon chaat masala
ground chilli and salt to taste

TO GARNISH
Small bowls of date and tamarind chutney and coriander chutney (page 89)
275g/10oz natural yoghurt, whisked until smooth
chopped coriander leaves
paprika
garam masala

Combine the potato, onion, chickpeas and moong bean sprouts with a good squeeze of lemon juice and season with chaat masala, chilli and salt. Spoon the mixture into a serving bowl and place on the table along with the garnish ingredients.

To serve the dahi puri, carefully poke a hole in the top of the puri shell and part-fill with the potato mixture. Add ½ teaspoon or so of date and tamarind chutney and coriander chutney and top with a teaspoon of yoghurt.

Garnish with coriander leaves, a shake of paprika and garam masala, pop into the mouth and enjoy immediately.

BHEL PURI

A zingy, crunchy mixture of sev, puffed rice, diced mango, potato, tomato and onion, combined with chutney and lemon juice.

SERVES 4–6

4 teacups puffed rice
1 largish waxy potato, peeled,
    diced and boiled until soft
half a medium-sized firm mango, diced
2 medium tomatoes, diced
half a medium red onion, diced
1 or 2 green chillies, finely chopped
a large handful of chopped coriander
    (plus extra to garnish)
75g/3oz peanuts
1 teaspoon dry roasted cumin powder
1 teacup sev (plus extra to garnish)

CHUTNEY DRESSING

5 tablespoons date and tamarind
    chutney (page 89), thinned
    with a little water to give a
    pouring consistency
3 tablespoons coriander chutney
2 tablespoons lemon juice
1 heaped tablespoon dry-roasted
    cumin powder
salt

Whisk the dressing ingredients together until well combined.

Dry-roast the puffed rice for a couple of minutes in a hot frying pan (this ensures it is really crispy). Allow it to cool a little and then combine with the remaining ingredients and the chutney dressing. Serve immediately garnished with extra sev and coriander.

Serve immediately garnished with a sprinkling of the reserved sev and coriander.

CHAAT MASALA

Chaat masala is the flavour that most characterizes Indian snacks. It adds zing to chaats and salads, and is even sprinkled onto cut fruit. Amchoor (dried powdered mango) and black salt (rock salt) defines its unique taste. Chaat masala is available ready made in Indian stores, or why not make your own?

3 tablespoons cumin seeds
2 tablespoons coriander seeds
1½ teaspoons black peppercorns
1 teaspoon fennel seeds

1 largish dried red chilli
2 tablespoons amchoor
2 teaspoons ground black salt
¼ teaspoon hing (asefortida)

Dry-roast the cumin, coriander, black pepper and fennel for a minute or so in a hot frying pan. Allow to cool a little, and then grind to a powder with the dried chilli.

Combine with the amchoor, black salt and hing and store in an airtight jar until needed.

BARBECUED CHILLI AND LIME SWEETCORN

As the sun sets makeshift barbecues set up shop on the sandy beach. Stallholders adeptly waft a square of cardboard to whip up the flames that lick the plump sweetcorn cobs to the perfect blackened shade. Once a cob has been chargrilled half a lime dipped into salt mixed with ground chilli is liberally rubbed over it.

Char whole sweetcorn cobs on the barbecue in summer, or place under a hot grill until evenly cooked cook on all sides. For maximum pleasure coat the cobs with a drizzle of melted butter after rubbing with chilli salt.

PER COB

1 sweet corn cob   half a lime
sea salt mixed with ground chilli to taste   melted butter

Remove the husk from the corn and grill until charred on all sides.
Dip the lime into the chilli salt and firmly rub over the whole surface of the corn.
Finish off with a drizzle of melted butter.

CUNNING CROCKERY

All this snacking could lead to an awful lot of litter and a surplus of wasteful packaging, but not in India. Banana leaves and bowls shaped from dried pendu leaves are used as crockery and then discarded to become perfect fodder for roaming cattle. Empty chai teacups, fashioned from sun-fired clay, are smashed on the ground and crushed underfoot to return to the earth from which they came, and unwanted newspaper is carefully cut and expertly rolled into convenient shapes to wrap snacks on the go.

CHILLI CHEESE TOASTIES

Melted cheese, coriander chutney and chilli, who can resist? Toasties are tailored to a customer's desires – 'more chilli, a little less chutney, some tomato please' – then popped into a well-used toasted sandwich iron and placed over hot coals until molten on the inside and golden on the outside. If you have a toastie maker dig it out. Alternatively toast the sandwiches under a medium-temperature grill. The art to the perfect toastie is to melt the cheese without burning the bread.

Bread can be brown or white and paneer (Indian cottage cheese) makes a pretty good alternative to cheddar. In India toasties are always served with tomato ketchup, but that decision is yours.

MAKES 4 TOASTIES

8 slices medium-sliced sandwich bread
soft butter
simple coriander chutney (page 89)
175g/6oz crumbled paneer or
    grated cheddar
2 or 3 green chillies (or to taste),
    finely chopped

½ red onion, finely chopped
1 medium tomato, diced (optional)
a handful of chopped coriander leaves
1 scant teaspoon chaat masala (or to
    taste)
salt and black pepper
tomato ketchup (optional)

Butter the bread slices on both sides. Spread 4 of the slices with coriander chutney to taste.

Combine the cheese, chillies, onion, tomato and coriander, and divide evenly between the pieces of bread that have been spread with chutney.

Season to taste with chaat masala, salt and pepper, top with the remaining pieces of buttered bread and grill under a medium-temperature grill until the cheese has melted and the bread is golden brown. Serve piping hot, with a squirt of ketchup on the side.

CALCUTTA KATHI ROLLS

In the hustle and bustle of Calcutta's streets, expectant punters wait patiently around simple stalls as Kathi rolls are expertly assembled. Calcutta's famous snack is concocted from a choice of spicy fillings topped with chutney and rolled inside a paratha coated with scrambled egg. This recipe is for paneer but strips of chicken breast or a julienne of mixed vegetables will work equally well. To make the chutney, follow the recipe for simple coriander chutney on page 89, adding a small bunch of mint and reducing the amount of coriander by half.

Traditionally kathi rolls are made with paratha (fried unleavened bread). Chapattis offer a lower-fat option.Both are easily available from supermarkets and Indian stores.

SERVES 4–6

3 tablespoons sunflower oil
I medium onion, thinly sliced
2 cloves garlic, crushed
2.5cm/1 inch piece fresh ginger root,
    peeled and grated
250g/8oz diced paneer
1 teaspoon ground cumin
1 teaspoon ground coriander
½ teaspoon turmeric
1 teaspoon garam masala
2 medium tomatoes, diced
butter

6 paratha or chapatti
4 medium free-range eggs, beaten
salt and black pepper

TOPPINGS
A selection of:
simple coriander and mint chutney
    (see note above)
thinly sliced red onion
thinly sliced lettuce
finely chopped green chilli
chaat masala
squeeze of lemon juice

First make the paneer filling. Heat the oil in a frying pan, and when it is hot add the onion, garlic and ginger and fry until soft. Add the paneer and stir-fy together until the cheese starts to brown. Add the spices and stir-fry for a minute or so before adding the chopped tomatoes. Continue to stir-fry until the tomatoes break down. Season with salt to taste.

To assemble the kathi roll, heat a small knob of butter in a frying pan, add a paratha (or chapatti) and cook for a minute or so. Flip it over and spoon 2 tablespoons of beaten egg on top. When the egg starts to set, flip the paratha again and cook for a couple of minutes longer (until the egg is firm). Flip the paratha once more and spoon a portion of the hot paneer mixture on top. Lift the paratha from the pan, add toppings to taste and tightly roll. Serve piping hot.

PAV BHAJI

Dramatically prepared on a huge flat griddle or *tava*, pav bhaji is the ultimate fast food, Indian style. Mixed vegetables are simmered in a thick potato and tomato masala gravy and served with toasted *pav* (soft bread rolls) smothered in butter. Rather like a spicy bubble and squeak, filling and easy to prepare, pav bhaji always makes a popular choice.

Pav bhaji spice mix is available ready-made from Indian stores or mix your own by combining 1 tablespoon garam masala with 1 teaspoon mango powder (amchoor), ½ teaspoon caraway seeds and ½ teaspoon fennel seeds.

SERVES 4–6

450g/1lb mashing potatoes,
  peeled and cubed
half a medium cauliflower,
  cut into small florets
3 medium carrots, diced
175g/6oz fresh or frozen peas
3 tablespoons ghee or butter
1 medium onion, diced
4 garlic cloves, crushed
1 medium green pepper, diced
1½ tablespoons pav bhaji spice mix

1 teaspoon ground chilli
½ teaspoon ground turmeric
450g/1lb tinned chopped tomatoes
salt

To serve: extra butter; 2 lemons cut into
  wedges; 1 medium red onion, diced;
  a large handful of chopped coriander
  leaves; 6 soft rolls, halved, toasted
  and buttered

Boil the potatoes in salted water until soft, drain (leaving a splash of water in the pan) and roughly mash until a lumpy texture forms.

Simmer the cauliflower, carrots and peas in salted water until just soft, drain and set to one side.

Melt the butter in a large wok, add the onion, garlic and green pepper and fry until soft. Add the spices and stir-fry for a further minute or so.

Add the chopped tomatoes and gently simmer until the sauce has thickened. Stir in the mashed potatoes, cooked vegetables and salt to taste. Gently simmer for 5 minutes, stirring regularly to prevent sticking.

Serve the pav bhaji topped with a knob of butter, a good squeeze of lemon juice and diced red onion and chopped coriander to taste. Mop up the moreish masala sauce with the hot toasted rolls.

LASSI

This creamy yoghurt-based drink is deliciously cooling on a humid day and can be made sweet with the addition of fresh fruit, rose water and cardamom, or savoury with salt, ground cumin and fresh mint. Traditionally the ingredients are pounded together with ice until frothy, then poured into bulbous terracotta tumblers to serve.

SALT LASSI

SERVES 4–6
500g/1lb 2 oz full-fat natural yoghurt
275ml/½ pint cold water
½ teaspoon ground cumin
salt

To serve: ice; garam masala; fresh mint leaves

Blend all the ingredients together in a food processor until frothy. Pour into glasses over ice and garnish with a pinch of garam masala and fresh mint leaves.

BANANA LASSI

To make a sweet fruity lassi, blend 3 ripe bananas (or fruit of your choice) in a food processor with 350g/10 oz full-fat natural yoghurt, 1 dessertspoon of honey, 1 tablespoon of rose water and ½ teaspoon ground cardamom, until smooth. Add 275ml/½ pint cold water and blend until frothy. Serve poured over ice.

ROVING PEDLARS

In busy markets, favourite viewpoints, temples and pilgrimage sites, in fact any location where prospective customers might gather or linger for a while, roving vendors weave their way through the crowds offering all manner of tiffin from baskets adeptly balanced on the head, makeshift carriers strung around the neck or on the handlebars of a rickety bicycle. From sunrise on the banks of the sacred Ganges River to sunset at the gates of the majestic Taj Mahal, smiling vendors beckon and draw you in with a smile and the promise of 'best home-made savouries and sweets on sale'.

MASALA PAPAD

Crunchy papadoms topped with a chilli and lemony tomato salad, an ideal accompaniment to milky lassi, or a cold glass of beer.

SERVES 4–6
THE SALAD
3 medium tomatoes, finely diced
one-third of a medium-sized cucumber, finely diced
half a smallish red onion, finely diced
Good squeeze of lemon juice
2 green chillies, finely chopped
a handful of chopped coriander leaves
½ teaspoon chaat masala
salt to taste
6 papadoms

Combine the salad ingredients and just before serving sprinkle over the papadoms. Devour immediately before the papadoms become soggy.

POTATO BONDAS

These round potato fritters are usually made very spicy indeed. If you prefer something a little less eye-watering, it might be wise to reduce the amount of chopped chilli!

SERVES 4–6

THE FILLING
900g/2lb potatoes,
    cooked and roughly mashed
4cm/1½ inch piece of ginger root,
    peeled and grated
6 spicy green chillies, finely chopped
a handful of coriander leaves, chopped
3 dessertspoons desiccated coconut
1 dessertspoon sesame seeds
juice of a lime

2 teaspoons honey
salt
2 tablespoons sunflower oil

FOR THE BATTER
6 tablespoons chickpea flour
1 teaspoon ground turmeric
1 teaspoon chilli powder
a good pinch of salt
sunflower oil for deep-frying

Combine all the filling ingredients together and shape by hand into balls about the size of a golf ball.

To make the batter, sift the chickpea flour into a bowl, make a well in the middle and gradually add a little water until a thick batter forms.

Heat enough oil to deep-fry the bondas (the oil is hot enough when a drop of batter sizzles). Dip 4 balls of potato mixture in the batter and deep-fry until golden brown all over. Repeat, frying in batches until all the bondas are cooked.

Drain the bondas on kitchen paper for a few minutes before serving.

TOASTED MIXED NUT AND POTATO PAWA

Pawa (dried flattened rice flakes) are mixed with toasted nuts, potatoes, herbs and spices in this unusual and nutritious dish. Topped with a dollop of natural yoghurt, it makes an excellent breakfast.

SERVES 4–6

2 medium-sized waxy potatoes,
   peeled and diced
110g/4oz pawa
3 tablespoons sunflower oil
1 teaspoon black mustard seeds
1 teaspoon cumin seeds
50g/2oz peanuts
50g/2oz cashew nuts
50g/2oz almonds
½ teaspoon ground turmeric
½ teaspoon ground chilli
8 curry leaves
1 green chilli, finely chopped
a handful of desiccated coconut
a handful of coriander leaves,
   roughly chopped
½ teaspoon golden caster sugar
salt
lemon juice

Simmer the diced potato in boiling water until soft. Drain the potatoes and set to one side.

Cover the pawa flakes with water, soak for 5 minutes, and then drain thoroughly.

Heat the sunflower oil in a large wok, add the mustard and cumin seeds and as the seeds start to pop add the nuts. Stir-fry until the nuts are toasted and golden.

Stir in the turmeric, ground chilli and curry leaves. Cook for a minute or so, then add the diced potato. Stir-fry until the potatoes are golden brown.

Add the chopped chilli and desiccated coconut. When the coconut starts to turn golden, add the drained pawa and gently stir-fry together until the pawa is heated through.

Stir in the chopped coriander, sugar and salt to taste. Serve hot with a good squeeze of lemon juice (and an optional spoonful of natural yoghurt).

FRESH FRUIT CHAAT

A sweet but savoury taste sensation: fresh fruit is dressed with orange and lime juice and sprinkled with chaat masala to create a tangy and refreshing fruit salad.

SERVES 4–6
2 bananas
1 mango
1 large apple
1 papaya
one-third of a pineapple
1 small pomegranate
the juice of a lime
2 tablespoons fresh orange juice
1 teaspoon chaat masala (see page 96)
1 teaspoon dry-roasted ground cumin

To garnish: a handful of fresh
    mint leaves

Peel the banana, mango, apple, papaya and pineapple and cut into bite-sized chunks. Cut the pomegranate into quarters, remove the seeds and combine with the fruit salad.

Dress the fruit with the lime and orange juice, sprinkle the chaat masala on top and gently mix together. Serve garnished with fresh mint leaves.

A DHABA PIT STOP

Dhabas, simple roadside cafés, offer home-style cooking at unbeatable prices, the perfect truck stop on a long journey. Welcoming and friendly, they were originally characterized by *chowpoys* (rope cots), where weary truck drivers could catch forty winks after a slap-up meal. A wooden plank placed across the *chowpoy* served as a makeshift table. Dhabas are rather more salubrious these days with neat and clean tables and chairs!

MASALA CHAI

Strong Assam tea is simmered with milk and mixed spices until scalding hot to make this aromatic milky tea. Masala chai is usually served tooth-achingly sweet in chai glasses or little clay cups, but of course you don't need to add that much sugar – the choice is yours. If you want to drink your chai like a local, pour it between two glasses until it froths up cappuccino style. Masala chai spice mix stores well in an airtight container for up to a month. I always keep a supply in the store cupboard.

FOR THE MASALA SPICE MIX
4 tablespoons ground black pepper
3 tablespoons ground cardamom
3 tablespoons ground ginger
2 tablespoons ground cinnamon
1 tablespoon ground cloves
1 tablespoon ground nutmeg

Place the spices in a container with a tight-fitting lid. Shake the sealed jar until the spices are well combined. Store in a dark cupboard until ready to use.

SERVES 4–6
275ml/½ pint full-fat milk
275ml/½ pint water
2 teaspoons masala spice
4 teaspoons Assam tea leaves
brown sugar to taste

Pour the milk and water into a milk pan and whisk in the masala spice. Heat together until bubbles start to form around the edge of the pan.
Add the Assam tea and gently simmer, stirring regularly, for a further 5 minutes.
Strain the tea into cups and add sugar to taste.

CHILLI PAKORA

For an authentic *dhaba* pit stop, team sweet masala chai with piping hot chilli pakora.

At *dhaba*s pakoras are skilfully fried in vast cauldrons of hot oil and served freshly cooked with date and tamarind chutney (page 89) for dipping. Back home they work just as well shallow-fried in sunflower oil.

Choose a chilli to suite your taste buds, just make sure they are large and if possible still have the stalk attached. Chickpea flour is available from Asian stores, health food shops and good supermarkets.

MAKES 12

12 large green chillies
75g/3oz chickpea flour (*besan*)
2 tablespoons rice flour
½ teaspoon ground turmeric

1 teaspoon cumin seeds
salt
sunflower oil

Slit the chillies down one side and carefully remove the seeds.

Combine the flours and spices in a bowl and gradually stir in enough warm water to make a thick pancake-style batter. Season the batter with salt to taste.

Heat a good glug of sunflower oil in a wok (the oil is ready when a drop of batter added to the oil sizzles). Using the stalk as a handle, coat 4 chillies in batter. Fry the coated chillies in the hot oil until golden brown on all sides. Repeat the process until all the chillies are cooked, adding extra oil when necessary.

Drain the cooked chilli pakora on kitchen paper before serving with date and tamarind chutney on the side.

KHASTA KACHORIS

Flaky pastry *khasta kachori* puffs filled with spiced lentils are made by the dozen at busy *dhabas*. The art to a good *kachori* is to fry the pastry until it is crisp, golden and puffed up.

To simplify things I always use ready-made rolled pastry. Mini *khasta kachoris* make excellent afternoon tiffin. Cut the pastry into 12 portions to make bite-sized puffs. And if you are looking for a snack a little lighter on the waistline, instead of frying, bake in an oven preheated to 200ºC/400ºF for 15–20 minutes, until golden brown.

MAKES 8

75g/3oz yellow split peas,
  soaked overnight
2 generous tablespoons ghee
  or butter
1 teaspoon cumin seeds
2 green chillies, finely chopped
3cm/1¼ inch piece ginger root,
  peeled and grated

1 teaspoon ground coriander
1 scant teaspoon ground turmeric
½ teaspoon cracked black pepper
salt
375g/14oz ready-made rolled
  shortcrust pastry
sunflower oil to fry

Drain the yellow split peas and set to one side.

Heat the ghee in a wok, add the cumin seed and as they start to splutter add the chilli and ginger and stir-fry for a minute or so.

Add the split peas and the remaining spices and stir-fry for a couple of minutes Add enough water to just cover the split peas and gently simmer until they are dry and just soft enough to roughly mash with the back of a spoon. Remove from the heat and set to one side to cool.

To assemble the *kachoris* unroll the ready-made pastry on to a wooden board and cut into 8 equal-sized portions, Divide the cooled split pea mixture between them.

Dampen the pastry edges with water and fold the pastry over the filling, stretching it a little as you do so. Pinch the edges together to make a rough ball shape, then use a rolling pin to gently flatten it into a patty.

Heat a good glug of sunflower oil in a wok. When the oil is really hot add 3 *kachoris*. Reduce the temperature to a low heat and fry the *kachoris* until they are golden brown and puffed up on both sides. Repeat the process until all the *kachoris* are cooked. Allow the *kachoris* to drain on kitchen paper for a few minutes before serving.

THE INDIAN COFFEE HOUSE CATERINGS AND BEVERAGES

The venerable Indian Coffee House has been the meeting place of poets, literati and revolutionaries for over fifty years. Run by a co-operative society, it is a favourite place for students and old-timers to exchange thoughts and views over a cup of Indian coffee and a snack. Immaculately turned out waiters, sporting white uniforms tied with dashing cummerbunds and topped with dramatic turbans, ceremoniously deliver trays of 'caterings and beverages' to packed tables in its lofty fan-cooled halls. Snacks have a vintage colonial feel. Boiled eggs, omelette, toast and jam share tables with stuffed paratha, pakora and biryani, and the 'espresso' comes milky and strong.

SPICED SOUTH INDIAN COFFEE

Mysore coffee brewed with cardamom and cinnamon, topped with a shot of hot frothy milk and a sprinkling of nutmeg. Traditionally generous spoonfuls of sugar are simmered with the coffee and spices to make a rather sweet brew, but of course you can add sugar to your own personal preference.

SERVES 6

I large cafétiere strong coffee
1 scant teaspoon ground cardamom,
1 cinnamon stick

brown sugar to taste
325ml/12fl oz full-fat milk
¼ teaspoon ground nutmeg

Pour the prepared coffee into a saucepan and combine with the ground cardamom and cinnamon. Add sugar to taste and simmer together for a few minutes to allow the spices to infuse with the coffee.

Meanwhile heat the milk and whisk until frothy.

Two-thirds fill heatproof glasses with the spiced coffee, top with frothy milk and sprinkle with nutmeg.

MASALA OMELETTE

Masala omelette makes a super-quick mid-morning snack or late breakfast. Serve Coffee House style with hot buttered toast.

PER OMELETTE
2 free-range medium eggs
1 tablespoon milk
2 shallots, finely chopped
1 green chilli, finely chopped
1 small tomato, finely diced
1 tablespoon chopped
   coriander leaves

a large pinch of ground turmeric,
   garam masala and ground
   black pepper
salt
butter to fry

Whisk the eggs and milk together until light and fluffy.

Stir in the remaining ingredients, seasoning with salt to taste.

Heat a knob of butter in a non-stick frying pan. When the butter starts to foam, add the omelette batter and swirl it around the pan until evenly coated.

Reduce the heat to a medium temperature and cook the omelette until golden brown and nearly set.

Flip the omelette and cook for a further minute (don't overcook the omelette at this stage or it will become rubbery), before turning out on to a warm plate.

STUFFED PARATHA WITH YOGHURT AND LIME PICKLE

Flaky pan-fried unleavened bread stuffed with a thin layer of chilli potato makes a classic elevenses coffee break special. Tear off a bite-sized piece of stuffed paratha and spoon a little yoghurt and lime pickle on top. Ready-made paratha and lime pickle are both readily available from Asian stores and good supermarkets, making this an easy dish to rustle up anytime.

FOR 4 PARATHA
3 tablespoons sunflower oil
1 teaspoon cumin seeds
2 medium potatoes, peeled and diced
2 or 3 finely chopped green chillies
2.5 cm/1 inch piece ginger root,
    peeled and grated
1 teaspoon ground turmeric
1 teaspoon ground coriander

1 medium tomato, diced
a small handful of coriander leaves,
    finely chopped
salt
4 ready-made paratha

To serve: 250g/9oz natural yoghurt,
    whipped until smooth; lime pickle

Heat the oil in a frying pan until sizzling hot. Add the cumin seeds and as they start to crackle add the potato, chilli and ginger. Stir-fry together until the potatoes start to soften.

Add the turmeric and coriander and fry for a minute or so before adding a splash of water. Continue to cook, adding extra splashes of water when necessary, until the potato is soft and the water has completely reduced.

Roughly mash the potato, stir in the chopped coriander and season with salt to taste. Set to one side while you prepare the paratha.

Cut the paratha in half and, with the aid of a sharp knife, prise open the cut surface to make a pocket (don't worry if the paratha breaks up a little – the potato will hold it all together). Spoon the potato mixture inside the pocket and firmly flatten together.

Heat a flat griddle or frying pan and toast the paratha on both sides until heated through.

Serve with natural yoghurt and lime pickle.

INDEX OF RECIPES

Frances Lincoln Limited
74–77 White Lion Street
London N1 9PF
www.franceslincoln.com

Bombay Lunchbox
Copyright © Frances Lincoln Limited 2014
Text © Carolyn Caldicott 2014
Photographs © Chris Caldicott 2014

Food styling by Carolyn Caldicott
Designed by Becky Clarke

First Frances Lincoln edition 2014

A catalogue record for this book is available
from the British Library.

978-0-7112-3383-6

9 8 7 6 5 4 3 2 1